The Flower Lady

And Other Short Stories, 2nd Edition

Frances W. Moss Moore

The Flower Lady

Copyright © 2011 by Frances W. Moss Moore

All rights reserved. No part of this book may be reproduced or transmitted in any form or by any means without written permission of the author.

Contributions by Joyce A. Barnes

Karol Brown, Editor

BROWN TONES PUBLISHING a subsidiary of

Lakewood, WA, USA
253-581-1954
www.browntonespublishing.com

ISBN 978-0-9840050-0-0

Library of Congress Control Number: 2012900172

Mrs. Nancy L. Webster • Our Mother

The Flower Lady

First Edition by Frances W. Moss Moore

Second Edition Dedicated to Frances W. Moss Moore

The Author of The *Flower Lady*

Our Mother

Introduction

By Joyce A. Barnes

As soon as I began reading *The Flower Lady* again after several years, I was struck by the easy elegance of the writing. Then I remembered that the writer is my own mother. Everywhere I go around town, people who know Frances Moss Moore tell me what a wonderful person she is. So generous, so kind, so giving, and some even know she is a gifted actress and speaker, having witnessed her recitals of Paul Lawrence Dunbar poems or appearances in local commercials. However, I doubt many realize what a wonderful writer she is. That may be because this book, first self-published in 1981, has remained mostly on the shelves and in the boxes of family members. It is fitting and good that her daughter Karol has republished *The Flower Lady* and made it available to a wider audience.

In some of these recollections, Mama recreates her life growing up with her parents, Matthew and Nancy Webster, her younger sister, Irene, and the relatives, teachers, and merchants in the coal mining towns of West Virginia and Kentucky. She paints her pictures with details and dialogue that take us back to a less hectic time. A time when vendors still called out their wares along the dirt roads. A time of one-room school houses. A time when a child could see the Appalachian Mountains from her front porch and take off one day to climb "the Big Rock." In other stories, she recounts her experiences as a young mother in post-War America. She chronicles the historic social and economic changes in Black people's lives through the experiences of her extended family. Her husband and precocious young son in Chicago. Her sister's family in Detroit. Her own parents, uncles, aunts, and cousins who also left the coal mining towns and limitations of the segregated "South" (Kentucky had been a slave state), for the big cities, white collar jobs, and expanding opportunities in places like Chicago, Detroit, and even Dayton. Finally, she continues the family stories up to her mother's 75th birthday, where a unique gift to "the Flower Lady" serves as a symbol of the family's growth, progress, prosperity, and blessings.

Now, on the occasion of her own 90th birthday, the original collection of stories has been augmented with photos, a family tree, and Frances's remembrance about "Going to the Big Rock," a story that reveals her early and enduring optimism, ambition, fearlessness, and willingness to take action even when there are risks. We can only hope she will continue to write about her own and her family's lives because she and her stories tell us all something about how to live.

Foreword

Although some of these incidents do not involve you directly, Mama, I hope you will enjoy remembering those days.

With Love,

"Frank"

Table of Contents

The Flower Lady 1
The Flower Lady's Tools 9
Use What You Got 10
Chickens for Rags 17
The Stranger Was Our Brother 19
Happy Birthday 23
First Flight 30
A Leash for Denny 32
Who Licked the Pickle? 38
Grandmother's Sayings and Courage 43
The Big Rock 54
Mr. and Mrs. Jessie Moore 58
Frances Webster Moss Moore 60
90th Birthday Party 66

The Flower Lady

She loved growing things and was surrounded by a wilderness of many different varieties of flowers, shrubs, vegetables, trees - anything that grows in the good earth. Pots of varying sizes and shapes lined the many shelves and windows of her home. It was the flower and garden showcase of her neighborhood. Those friends and neighbors who shared her love for these things were known to get out of bed to come and witness the splendor of a night blooming wonder called the "Babe in the Manger," as this occurrence was thought to be quite rare.

Through some means, she learned how to wrap a piece of yarn around a pencil, execute a few dips and turns, pull the yarn through some of the loops, and the results was a flower, the design somewhat like a four-leaf clover. These she would make in red and white and sell for 25 cents each on Mother's Day. For a housewife in the rugged, bleak, mountain hamlet of a coal mining community, the sale of these simple cuties was a whopping profit. This humble beginning of artificial flower making was the nucleus of what was to become a lifetime of devotion to this craft that would reveal an artistic imagination to rival the works of many who had professional training and guidance of many years.

A move to another coal mining community spawned the occasion for her to meet and get to know Professor Drowley. He was a man of many talents. Besides being a teacher in the public school system, he was also a concerned citizen who delighted in imparting knowledge not only to the children of this backwoods little village, but to the parents as well. He was recruited from one of the larger cities of the state and thereby he represented "culture" that was unknown in the remote areas. So when Professor Drowley announced that he would teach a class in crepe paper magic, it went unheeded, except for three or four young women who dropped out after the first class. It was considered to be big city nonsense, with no apparent practicality here. But one young lady remained. And the good professor proudly instructed her as conscientiously as he would have done for a room full of students because he instinctively knew that this young woman possessed the qualities that led to the success of whatever she chose in her mind to accomplish. Along with her natural ability, her eagerness to learn, her inquisitiveness and her ambition and ingenuity, here was a diamond in the rough that time would polish to a dazzling brilliance.

She quickly mastered the art, and after only a brief period of in-struction was turning out beautiful creations in all the colors of the rainbow. These crepe paper imitations were long and short stemmed roses, carnations, and many other of the familiar flowers that were known to all.

Salesmanship, too, .seemed to be one of her natural attributes, so it was not long before she had "a little change" coming in from sales to the townspeople whose homes were decorated with bouquets held in fancy bottles and various holders that served as vases. This somewhat steady flow of revenue, though small in amount, was put to good use. It helped to provide some of the necessities for a family that consisted of two young daughters whom she was determined to motivate to stay in school and escape the stagnation that was inevitably a part of the life of the coal miner's child bride.

From reading an advertisement, she learned that a company in Chicago that sold materials for artificial flower making gave free lessons with a purchase of a certain amount of money. At the first opportunity that presented itself, she found herself on State Street looking for the address of the establishment. She introduced herself, spent all of two days there, and returned home with new vigor and in possession of an innovative method for making roses. They were made by using a little box that had a hole in the top shaped like a doughnut. The material used was called "Wood Fiber" and was soft and velvety to the touch. These roses were so lifelike they had to be felt in order to see if they were the real thing.

Of course, this new discovery made it possible for her to produce more in a shorter time. Also, she deftly designed beautiful corsages, which in time would become the trademark of her flower-making career.

The artificial rose corsages were snubbed at first by the so-called elite and the connoisseurs (her clientele now was more select, having moved some time ago to a large city). However, when the reputation of the flowers was noised about how fresh they remained weeks, months, and even years, with proper storage, corsages from the *"Flower Lady"* was a sought after commodity. Churches and clubs as well as individuals wanted large orders of corsages and special arrangements for their noteworthy days and occasions. Sales grew into the $100 range, which was a gigantic boost from the small change days of her early endeavors.

For the *"Flower Lady,"* the contacts and friends she made were as important as the money. She considered making flowers a hobby which was thoroughly enjoyed. But she was just as happy when she was teaching others to "work their fingers" for she was a congenial, God fearing, life-long devoted Christian. She was not selfish with her gift and she readily encouraged anyone who wanted to learn to come to her home to be taught. Her biggest regret was that neither of her daughters was interested in learning the craft. Their talents, they felt, had yet to be discovered. Her grandchildren seemed to show a bit more interest than their mothers, but they were so busy holding down jobs and rearing their young children that they did not have much time to spare for this activity.

Although the *"Flower Lady"* has taught classes at her home, at the YWCA, the Senior Citizen Center, and various other places, no one seems as adaptable to this art as she. So she is still sought by many when an occasion calls for a certain bit of whimsy that she is known to be able to whip up without any hesitation. For a few years now, she has vowed to give it all up. But she will admit that flower making became a way of life for her without realizing what was happening. It is doing something that she enjoys and if it were in her power, she would not change it. So at the age of 81, the *"Flower Lady,"* my mother, is still young, sparkling with vitality, and going strong.

The Rose made of Wood Fiber*

Ribbon Rose Buds*

A 2011 version of the Chrismas Corsage*

Grandmother with a Christmas Corsage

Grandmother wearing a Carnation

Carnation made with Wood Fiber

The Flower Lady's Tools

Grandmother passed on her love for floral design. All of her 10 grand children and any neighbor children that were interested had an opportunity to learn to make flowers. One granddaughter carried on the tradition, K.V. The Flower Lady's tools were pinking Shears, wood fiber, wrapped wire, handmade patterns, a crafty inventive little flower box and floral tape.

The corsages in this book are samples of the flowers Grandmother taught KV to make. Using the rare and cherished wood fiber, pinking sheers and other tools Grandmother once used.

*Made by Karol (KV) Moss Brown, October, 2011.

Use What You Got

When Moses went down to Egypt
To lead the Israelites....
The Lord said, "What's that in your hand?
Use what you got"

This is an excerpt from a tattered, dog-eared little book that Mama had and used often. From this, she selected pieces for us to recite on special programs. The origin of this little publication is not known to this writer, nor do I remember the authors of the selections that were offered therein. In retrospect, I now know that it was written in what was called "dialect," somewhat on the order of Paul Lawrence Dunbar's works. Anyway, these little gems were full of wit, advice, and wisdom.

Being little girls of six and seven or somewhere thereabouts, we abhorred the times we had to memorize a "speech" from that little beat up book because that meant standing on a stage in the little one-room church (that was also our schoolhouse) and reciting for an audience of grown folks. However, in spite of not wanting to do this, one of those readings from the book has been remembered through all of these years and has had a remarkable impact on my life. It is the one from which the excerpt above is taken whose title I have chosen for this dissertation about Mama.

Mama is a perfect example of one who put to good use the abilities that she possessed. She had very little formal education, but this was a mind that was not wasted. For the most part, her generation of children growing up poor in the Deep South meant picking cotton and chopping weeds and the sundry other chores that had to be done by the children as well as the adults. Attendance at school was only for a short time in the brief winter months. At other times, they were in the fields.

Mama remembers passing to the fourth grade. By that time, she was old enough to work full time, so along with the multitude of other Negro children, that was the end of schooling.

It is my belief that some are blessed to have been born with initiative and motivation. Mama's parents had not the opportunity to go to school at all. Grandma, (Angeline Smothers) was born the year of "Surrender," 1865.

By some means, Grandma learned to read her Bible. I don't believe she could write. Perhaps this fact helped to inspire Mama to spend long hours at night by the kerosene lamp practicing how to write over and over again. The result of this dogged determination is a beautiful specimen of penmanship that one would consider to be the product of a well-educated scholar. The basics that she learned in the few months she spent in school were used to the maximum. She put to good use what little knowledge she had. She used what she got.

Religion played a major part in the lives of Negro people of that era (as it does now, but not to that extent). Much of the knowledge that was acquired was through the church or church-related activities. So it was natural, I suppose, for Mama to become an ardent church worker. And due to the fact that she possessed such a beautiful handwriting, she was repeatedly called upon to serve as the secretary for the various meetings. She very ably recorded with accuracy and her dependability and conscientiousness caused her to be recognized as a very intelligent, likeable, and valuable person. Her reading skills were good, as well as her comprehension of things. So she very gradually, but surely developed and maximized what she had acquired along the way.

Along with other things, Mama, all throughout the years, has taught Sunday School, worked and taught in the Missionary Society authoritatively and ably. She has numerous certificates that she earned through Bible study, attendance at conventions and congresses and many other sources that she availed herself of. She even attended night classes in English to help her to use the proper form of speech, which was put to good use because she has been called upon on many occasions to speak on special programs. Her audience never ceases to be amazed when she verbalizes that her formal education was so limited in scope. Along with her self-help, she likes to give credit to her children, who she said, helped her. The fact that we had the privilege of graduating from high school was always a source of pride for her and Daddy. Twelve years of school, nine months out of a year was quite an accomplishment in their eyesight!

"Use what you got" also carried over into Mama's kitchen. Often our cupboard was bare to the extent that it seemed impossible that someone could put together a decent meal for a family of four. But even though I can remember suppers that consisted of cornmeal dumplings (delicious) or hot water cornbread and wild greens, I don't remember being hungry, with absolutely nothing to eat. Mama would say, "Eat it anyway. Once your stomach is full, it won't care whether it's salt pork or steak."

These are just a few examples of occasions that help me to remember that old reading "Use What You Got." Since becoming an adult, I have had to rely on my resources for the situation at hand and make the most of what was currently there. I am sure that Mama would be surprised to know that most of the time when this occurred my mind would automatically turn back to the little old book and say, "Use what you got".

I later learned from Mama the author's name and the city from which she ordered the book. She also recited the reading "Use What You Got" in its entirety. The reading follows on the next page.

Frances Webster and Irene Webster

4 generations of taking part in church programs

Use What You Got

(A Poem written in "Dialect")

When Moses went down in Egypt
To lead the Israelites
He headed for the Promised Land
But saw some curious sights
When he got down to that Red Sea
He gave up on the spot
The Lord said, "What's that in your hand?
Use what you got"
He long had lugged that heavy rod
As shepherds always do
But never had he figured out
It would open water too.
To kill a snake, or walk a log
It helped him out a lot
Now save 600 thousand men?
Use what you got
The wilderness was on each side
Old Pharaoh's host behind
That big Red Sea stretched out in front
No bridge of any kind
His faith got weak, he prayed for help Lord, will I fail or not?
The Lord said, "What's that in your hand?"

Use What You Got

Use what you got"
Now listen, folks, this is a fact
You can believe it if you please
Most of us sometime in life
Get between the gun and seas
But if you bear this in mind
It works out on the dot
You pray for things right in your hands
Use what you got
It's true that some must burn at stake
And some must withstand a shot
But as long as Jesus backs you up
Use what you got.

By: William E. Dancer A. Black poet of Jacksonville, FL

Chickens for Rags

Mama was never one to pass up a bargain, so when this unusual sales exchange seemed in the making she eagerly got ready to pounce upon it.

Quite frequently, vendors hawking their vast array of goods would come to the people in these out of the way coal mining communities and they were greeted enthusiastically. The small grocery store, with an even smaller amount of household items, etc. was quite a little distance to walk, so these "peddlers" as they were called, had a thriving business among the hill people. Their bolts of fabric, pictures, and bric-a-brac provided an outlet for browsers, as well as a convenience for those who had the money to buy.

On this particular occasion, a peddler came with what Mama thought was a very worthwhile, very different, most interesting twist. She could hear him faintly in the distance as he slowly made his ascent on the Hill, stopping often for customers to be accommodated. The closer he came, the more she was sure of what, at first, she simply thought that she had heard afar off.

"Chickens for rags, chickens for rags," intoned the man in the sing-song nasal twang peculiar to natives of the hill country. Mama sprang into action. "I have plenty of rags. C'mon, children, let's get busy and get them together. We should be able to get up enough to get at the least, two, or maybe even three chickens," she chuckled happily. Mama waited anxiously until the vendor finally arrived in front of our house. Looking him directly in the eye, she was ready to drive a hard bargain.

"How many rags do you want per chicken?" The man stared at her with a puzzled expression. "What are you talking about, lady?"

"All the way up here you were yelling "chickens for rags, chickens for rags. Okay, how many rags do you want per chicken?"

Guffaws spontaneously broke out among everyone standing around the peddler's cart. The peddler, himself was bent over in un-controllable laughter. Mama looked from one to the other, bewildered. Then suddenly the explanation for all of this explosion of mirth hit her and she too burst out laughing. Between peals of laughter, the man repeated slowly and distinctly the words he was actually saying. "I was calling out "chickens or aigs, chickens or aigs". That was a long, long time ago. But it is still one of our favorite family jokes.

Aunt Mary, Grandmother's sister and Grandmother
"Chickens or aigs"

The Stranger Was Our Brother

Sister Earlene and I had practically finished the wash and were hurriedly hanging the clothes on the clotheslines to dry. Our attention was suddenly diverted by the figure of a man in the distance. He had turned and was coming up the back alley. Our curiosity was only slightly aroused because our immediate goal was to hurry up and finish the laundry, a chore that we thoroughly disliked, and get down to the vacant lot where the kids were already playing "Soakum." As always on washday, we were in a sour mood. Not only did we have to do the family wash, but also the terribly soiled clothes of a bachelor cousin of Mama's. This was to be only until he could find a permanent washwoman, which could not be too soon for us. Our hands always had broken skin from the hard rubbing on the washboard.

So it was this unpleasant frame of mind that pervaded when the strange man, who had made his way up the alley, turned into our yard. We stared at him with belief. He was just about the most peculiar person we had ever seen. Immediately, we saw that he was not old, maybe about 17 or 18. But to a nine year old and an eight year old, that was kind of old. He had what seemed to us an over-sized mouth that housed huge white teeth. His eyes were a reddish brown and they darted amusingly from one of us to the other. The man's clothes, though clean, hung on him loosely and I immediately thought of the picture of the scarecrow that I had seen in my Agriculture schoolbook. Or, I thought, as Earlene and I stood immobile on the spot, he could be compared to the comics section character "Pete-the-Tramp" (a name that was subsequently to stick with him throughout the years).

But the most astonishing thing, aside from his appearance in general, was the stranger's right forearm - missing up to the elbow! Again wild thoughts raced through my head. Could this be a pirate who had been at sea and maybe the Captain of the ship cut off his arm? All the more reason to wonder why he chose our back yard to stop. Oh, he was probably just looking for a handout of food or a drink of water or something, I theorized in my mind.

Even as we were sizing him up (negatively), the strange young man was also giving us the once over, still with that enormous mouth spread in that huge grin that showed his great big teeth.

"Wish he would say what he wants and be gone," I thought. Anyway, what was so funny about us - he was the one who looked as though he was a refugee from the pages of a comic book.

Finally, he spoke. "Maffew Wesson liv here?"

Wow! In addition to his way-out appearance, he couldn't talk either. His was the worst of Southern accents that we had ever heard (not new to us as our parents and relatives were from the Deep South); and what a slaughter of the English language!

We nodded in the affirmative.

"Then you guls mus be Francene and Erlene," the grin stretching even broader, if that were possible. Dumbfounded, we again nodded "Yes." How did he know this, we puzzled. Maybe he wasn't just a hobo after all, but maybe he was a "prophet" like that "Prophet Jeremiah" that had stopped through here recently and had frightened everybody with his terrible prophecies. We'd better try to be nice to him or he might foretell doom for us.

Erlene, the brave one, regained her composure first and asked. "Who are you and what do you want?"

Imagine our consternation when the strange, ill-clothed, no talking, cut-off arm, big mouth, grinning man, seemingly relishing each word he spoke said, "Ya neva seen me befo. My nam is Wally Jo Wezzer, Maffew Wezzer's son.

I yo bruzzer"

Brother Willie James

top: Irene, Matthew, *middle:* Frances, Irene, Nancy
bottom: Frances and Nancy Webster

Happy Birthday

My sister is usually the one who thinks of innovative ways to commemorate the special days such as Christmas, Mother's Day, and birthdays. It was her idea to have a surprise family get-together for Mama on her 75th birthday. The really big surprise would be to have our nearest and dearest cousin (she is thought of more as one of Mama's sisters and as our aunt), who lives in Detroit to be present for the occasion. Also, we would make arrangements for the event to be featured in *Pride Magazine*, a prominent, pictorial, local publication of which the Black community is quite proud.

So on March 7, 1975, all of our children and grandchildren, long-time family friends, and our Detroit relatives gathered en masse at 37 North Ardmore, Sister's home of lo these many years and waited anxiously for Mama to return home from church. She was making her home with Sister after selling her own house and before she moved to the Senior Citizens' High Rise.

Finally, the long waited for time arrived and when Mama entered the door, she was swept off her feet with a roaring "SURPRISE, SURPRISE - HAPPY BIRTHDAY." The impact was so sudden that for a moment she was speechless. But as everyone began to converge upon her and she recognized what was happening, the tears burst forth. But short-lived, because now everyone was laughing, singing, gloating over the perfectly kept secret, and most especially the one about the Detroiters.

Now it was time for everyone to help himself to the delicious turkey and ham with all the trimmings dinner that all of the children

Dedication

Dear Mama, Happy 90th Birthday, We are so blessed to have you in our lives. "You Light Up Our Lives" We Love You.

Kenny, Karol, Johnny, Joyce

Frances Moore's 75th Birthday Party December 1996
Joyce, Frances, Karol, Kennth, John, sitting Nancy Webster

highest. She was settling down to play a game of 'UNO" with the grand-children when we summoned her to the living room for our "Ace In the Hole".

It was then that we unveiled the money tree. "Ohhhhhhhhhh," she exclaimed. "How sweet it is - all of that good ice cream and cake plus this big bouquet of flowers. You shouldn't have done it." At the urging of all of us to "take a closer look," she did, and could not hold back the floodgate of tears. She was just overcome with emotion at the sight of the money tree. She had thought it was really a bouquet of flowers. Every time she would try to absorb the impact of the very thought, and the idea, and the planning, as well as the actual making of the tree, she would start crying again. When she was finally calm enough to talk, she wondered how in the world did we do it. Although she was the "Flower Lady," she had not seen anything quite like this the dollar bills shaped to look like flowers! She vowed not to dismantle it before all of her friends at the Center had had a chance to admire it.

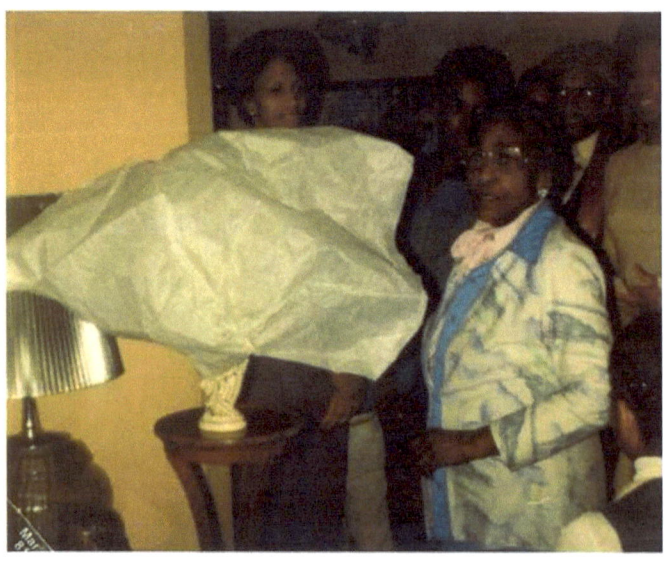

Happy Birthday

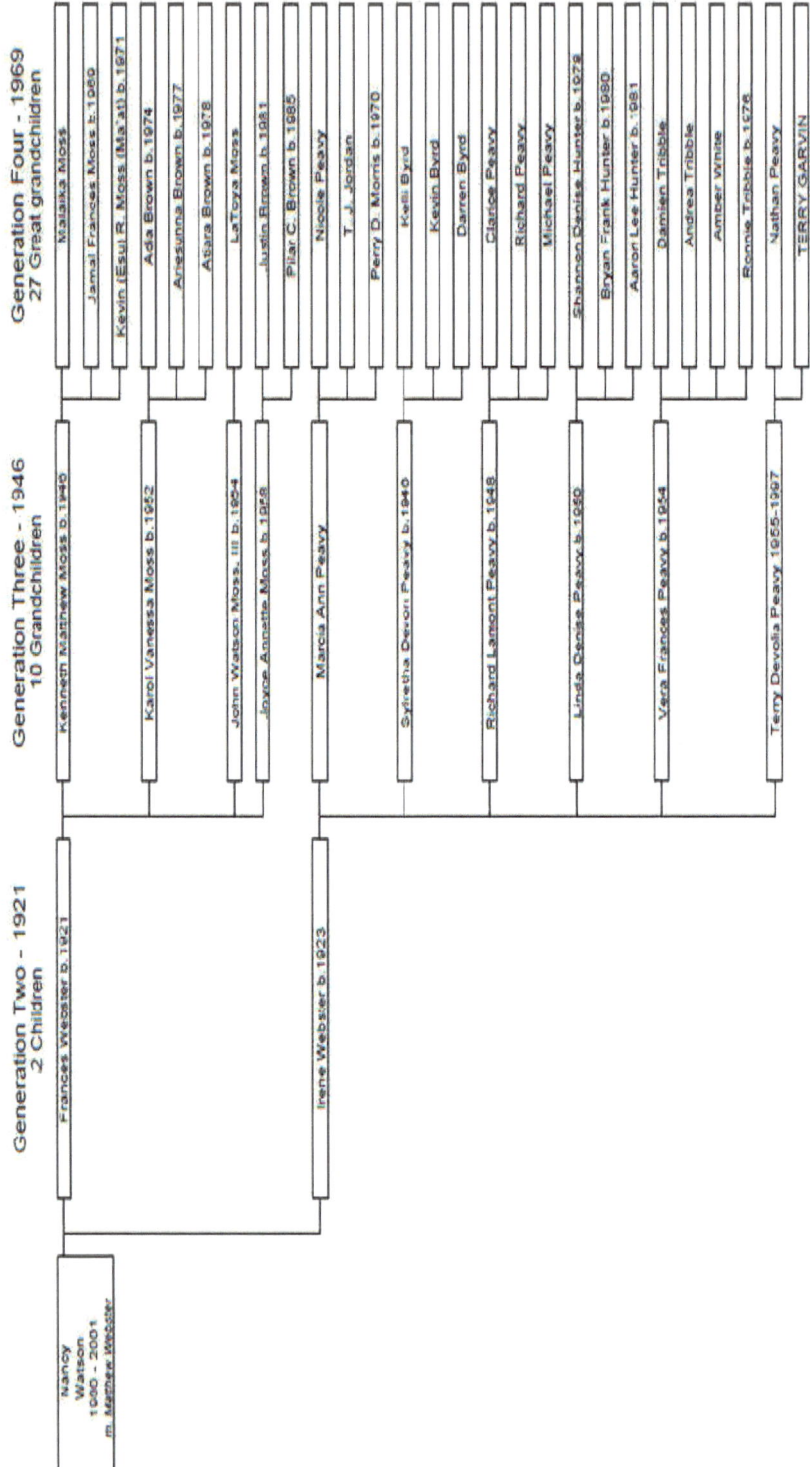

First Flight

I suspect that the main reason Mama consented was the fact that this would be a chance for her to visit her childhood friend and relative who for many years had been imploring her to come to Los Angeles for a visit. So it was this "Achilles' Heel" that I aimed for in order to get her to say "yes" she would go with us as a tour group to Los Angeles by air. The occasion was the graduation and marriage of my youngest child, who had completed her four years at the University of Southern California and in addition to that, she was getting married. So at the age of 80, in June 1980, Mama took her first trip by airplane.

While we waited with the other members of the tour troupe, Mama was quite herself, stepping about spritely, and making the acquaintances. Smartly attired in a stylish pantsuit, no one would have guessed her age. She looked very much like the rest of the mature ladies (only one man went along) in the group. She was calm, showing no sense of foreboding or apprehension, which could not be said of many who are about to board a flying machine into the wild blue.

Our seats were in two's, so Sister sat with a group of three and I sat with Mama, so at least if her calm gave away, she would not be seated beside a stranger. As we coasted up the runway and gradually, lifted farther and farther off terra firma, I furtively glanced out of the corners of my eyes at her to see how she was reacting.

She was sitting upright, very still, staring straight ahead. I knew instinctively that she was sending up a prayer that her faith in His protection would be confirmed by providing a safe trip. After that, she relaxed and settled back, ready to enjoy the lunch that was being prepared as well as to be enthralled by all the nuances of airplane travel such as the deftness of stewardesses, the serving of drinks, movies, etc.

An enjoyable week was spent with her friend, mostly reminiscing. We also took her sightseeing. Of all of the exciting and intriguing things that we saw, I believe the most memorable for Mama were the Jack LaLanne Studio (she was a long-time devoted exercise fan) and the streets "Hollywood and Vine" which brought back memories of another of her old-time favorites, Tom Brenneman and the Breakfast Club. Brenneman's kiss on the forehead has for many, many years been established as one of her "trademarks".

The return trip was equally as uneventful as far as flying goes. Everyone was just amazed at how well she weathered her first flight. She now very nonchalantly boasts that it just like riding in a car - only better. And she hastens to add, "The good Lord who looks after us on the ground also takes care of us in the air."

A Leash for Denny

It was about the time that Denny was six months old that we began to think that this, our first born, might be a bit different from the average child. Those were the days of the Campbell Soup commercials on radio that went "Um-m-m-m Good!" We thought it was cute and comical to watch Denny sitting in his crib rocking to the cadence of the tune, and although not yet able to talk, babbling in baby language in perfect time with the words of the commercial "Um-m-m-m da!"

This was only a beginning of much more to come, for when he did learn to talk he never missed an opportunity to do so, often to the embarrassment of his parents. Denny seemed to be totally without fear and would charm and awe strangers whom he would engage in conversation. Once I ventured into one of Chicago's exclusive boutiques that ordinarily I would pass up. After he was retrieved from his investigation of the fitting rooms, which he did by crawling under the curtains that separated the cubicles, and from in and out of the racks of dresses, Denny amused the sales clerks with his animated chattering. I emerged from the dressing room just as he was telling them "I eat rats." From the shocked looks on those proper and prim matrons, I knew it was futile to try to explain that this was one of the many spontaneous figments that originated who knows where.

We still chuckle about the time my sister and her four small children, and Denny and I were out for a car ride and Sister, lest we not find any, spelled out "I would really like to have some I-C-E- C-

R-E-A-M." Immediately Denny piped, "I want some ice cream, too." This was not unusual to me, as I knew that Denny could spell big words like refrigerator, as well as his name and his street. But it evoked peals of laughter from the others in the car.

Denny was about two years when his daddy was hospitalized after an accident on the job. When we visited him in the hospital, Denny would take his ABC's book and captivate an audience of nurse; patients, and of course, his daddy as he would read through the book, ad libbing after each alphabet with such phrases as "I lub you" when he read "V" is for valentine. When his daddy was discharged. Denny was a celebrity at the hospital. Everyone was referring to a cigarette as a "cig-a-sot" - Denny's pronunciation.

My biggest surprise, I think, was the first time he started naming off the different makes of cars as we rode on the streetcar one day. Denny was on his knees looking out of the window and began to name Ford," "Chevy," "Oldsmobile", etc. People asked, "Did you teach him this?" I did not, as I was as shocked as they were. Denny told them that his daddy taught him.

Along with Denny's super mental activity was an over abundance of physical activity, too. The only time he wasn't in motion was when he was asleep - a peaceful time for me. My sister swears that Denny was the cause of her little daughter, same age as he, to start walking when she did. We went to visit them in Detroit. Lolitha would stand holding on to the sofa, but would not let go and walk. Denny, who had started walking several months earlier, would rush up to her menacingly, imitating his favorite TV personality, Milton Berle, and his "I'll kill you a million times" line. In order to escape this little terror, Lolita let go of the sofa and scurried to safety as fast as her fat legs would carry her.

A day at the amusement park with Denny would make one vow never again to go in another one. Most of the kids would ride happily and serenely, with little squeals of delight. Not Denny. He would literally commandeer the airplane, or the car, or the merry-go-round, or what ever and demand all ownership rights by protesting loudly when it was time to get off the ride. To get him off a ride one had to use force, for he would kick, scream, and fight, drawing curious stares of everyone within sight. Some were amused; others felt, I am sure, that a few whacks in the right places would have been appropriate.

Once a comment was overheard that "they need to get a leash for that spoiled brat", which at one time I was prompted to do. Somehow, I felt inhumane holding him on a leash, so I abandoned this after a very short time.

There's no doubt that everyone felt that I needed a leash for Denny the day he wanted to drive the trolley bus in Dayton, Ohio. This was a new mode of transportation for Denny, as in Chicago we always rode the streetcar. So when the driver of the trolley had to leave the vehicle for a minute to attend to a problem on the outside, Denny got into the driver's seat and took command. No amount of cajoling or coaxing could make him budge from this spot. Knowing from experience the unnerving scene that would surely accompany all of this, I conveniently looked out of the window as though I was not aware of what was going on, leaving the resolving of this to my hapless mother. Somehow, she finally won out! But the bus driver and many of the passengers were not long amused when precious time was lost because of the episode.

There were many of these occasions that made me want to hide and take cover in the nearest shelter; like the time we went to visit a friend in another city. Sara was showing me around her new home - all beautiful and sparkling, everything in perfect order. When she led me into her master bedroom, quick as a flash, Denny darted from behind, plumped himself in the middle of the bed, and just lay there with his hands tucked behind his head, grinning mischievously. I could only try to apologize for this bizarre behavior and surmise that "the devil made him do it."

Finally, this one grand incident his father and I said will be Denny's nemesis. We were returning to Chicago on the train after vacationing in Dayton. As usual, it was impossible to keep Denny in his seat. After becoming weary of jumping up to run and get him so that he would not wander too far away we thought, oh well, that big boy that's coming down the aisle for a drink of water at the fountain will frighten him back to his seat. Sure enough, the big boy did command gruffly to Denny as Denny stood in the aisle blocking him, "Get out of my way, little boy, I'm thirsty." To which Denny coolly retorted, "No you're not - I'm Thursday, you're Wednesday", and proceeded to activate the fountain with his foot in order to get a drink for himself. People found it hard to believe that he was only four years old.

John, Frances and Kenny Moss

Who Licked the Pickle?

"I AM YOUR NEW TEACHER:

MY NAME IS MISS JULIE PRESS!"

We knew right away from her expression and by the determined and forceful way she wrote this message on the blackboard that she was no cream puff who could be pushed around and talked back to. Her predecessor, mousy little Miss Hannah Lee, was literally run out of the little one-room schoolhouse by one of the older fifth grade students. Miss Lee had attempted to punish the girl by making her wash the blackboard for disruptive behavior. She was obstinate and simply refused to do it. When Miss Lee walked up to her and demanded that she do it, Marva, our biggest student, and the worst troublemaker, got up out of her seat and gave the teacher a hard push that sent her toppling over two or three desks. The students, although awed by such audacity, could not restrain the giggles, and the utterly embarrassed Miss Lee scrambled to her feet and ran weeping out of the door. She did not come back the next day, nor ever.

To us, first grade to fifth grade students, it was a mystery how they found this new lady so quickly to fill the position vacated by the flight of Miss Lee. But she appeared the next day and her message via the blackboard was our official introduction.

Instinctively, we felt that, if nothing else, we were in for some excitement with Miss Press. We wondered who would be the first one to have an encounter with her. Finally, it happened. But strangely enough, the incident did not occur in the classroom, but during the lunch hour of about the second week after the arrival of the new teacher.

Miss Press rang the bell which signaled dismissal for lunch and proceeded to the little hallway to hand out the little half-pint bottles of milk, which those who were fortunate enough to have a nickel received. Those of us who had packed lunches clutched our enameled pails in one hand and held the milk bottle proudly in the other each saying as the milk was given to us, "Thank you, Miss Press".

Valerie Ware, a large for her age fifth grader, who almost never had the nickel to buy milk, was stopped as she passed by the teacher.

"Valerie, please go to the store and pick up some lunch for me," Miss Press said.

"Yes, Miss Press."

Of course, Valerie was pleased to do this little chore because the person who was chosen to go to the store for the teacher's lunch was always rewarded with a dime.

The little grocery store was only about a ten-minute walk from the school. It served as the community's all-purpose building, as dry goods (as we called everything that was not edible) were kept as well as groceries and meats. We enjoyed going there as it provided us with a chance to see some of the novelties and pretty items that were displayed on the counters and in the glass-enclosed casings. So those who had not been chosen so far were a bit envious of Valerie as she skipped happily on her way to the store with Miss Press' order.

After a short time, Valerie returned with the bologna, buns, and pickle for Miss Press' lunch. This was more or less standard fare, as restaurants had not reached this part of the coal mining hill country.

Valerie collected her reward and had started out of the door when she was stopped in her track by an urgent, markedly irritated summons by Miss Press. "Valerie, COME BACK HERE!"

On the outside, our ears perked up. Something was wrong. Our anticipation of some impending excitement was keen and this just might be it. And so it was.

Valerie's heart sank. How could she have known? Certainly, it would not show. Something else must not be in accordance with what Miss Press wanted. These thoughts raced frantically through her head as she turned and retraced her steps toward Miss Press.

"ARE YOU SURE THIS IS A DILL PICKLE? IT LOOKS TOO SMALL TO BE DILL!"

"Yessum, I'm sure."

"OH - AND HOW CAN YOU BE SO SURE - DID YOU TASTE THE PICKLE?"

"No, Mama. I didn't taste the pickle. But the butcher licked it to see if it was a dill pickle."

Valerie trembled visibly. She was not going to mention this to Miss Press. She knew that her word against the big White Authority which the butcher represented would mean nothing. And to have challenged him then and there when he did it was unheard of, this being many, many years before the Civil Rights era. Although in our little segregated hamlet we had never witnessed any of the outright inhumane treatment of Negroes by the white people, we heard of such atrocities from our parents. So we children never talked back to our parents; to this white butcher - never!

The "spies" that had the nerve to creep up to the door and look inside to get a first-hand glimpse of what was going on reported that the look on Miss Press' face was fury unlimited. She was so mad that even though she was of medium brown complexion, her color changed to an ashen grey.

Valerie began to cry. Even though she had been envied earlier by the students, she now had everyone's sympathy.

Miss Press grabbed the paper bag and its contents up from her desk and stalked angrily out of the schoolhouse.

"Never mind, Valerie. Stop that silly crying. I will handle this. Georgia, ring the bell at one o'clock and take the names of those who get up out of their seats or who talk while I am gone." She uttered all of this in one breath.

One can surmise that everything was quiet and orderly while Miss Press was away. No one wanted to be on the firing line when she returned.

Different versions were given of what actually happened at the store when Miss Press stormed in and confronted the butcher. Word-of-mouth reports supposedly witnessed by some of the mothers of the students was that Miss Press threw the sack with the bologna, buns and pickle on the counter and accused the butcher of licking it and demanded her money back. Another was that he denied licking the pickle and said that Valerie must have licked it herself. A more salacious version was that Miss Press grabbed the man and was about to beat him up, but was restrained.

Although the truth was never really confirmed as to what really happened, this was grist for the conversation and rumor mill both among the adults and school children as well for a long time. But I suppose the mystery of who actually licked the pickle will remain unsolved forever.

An old building from around the area during this time period

Grandmother's Sayings and Courage

Grandmother had two favorite expressions that she used to sum up the joys and sorrows experienced in the lives of her family and friends. If the event was a happy one, or a cause for jubilation, she would sing out "How sweet it is!"(borrowed from the popular comedian Jackie Gleason); if the occasion was sorrowful or troublesome, she would very calmly say "They are just going through their 'Garden of Gethsemane.' Everything will work out fine in the end."

It was this attitude of complete calmness and what seemed to be an apparent lack of empathy that was often puzzling to me, especially when everyone else concerned was distraught and upset. I wondered how grandmother. So kind-hearted understanding and helpful most of the time. Could remain detached and unperturbed when things were in turmoil. It was many years later when at age 84. Grandmother faced a crisis in her life that the answer appeared to me clearly and distinctly.

On the day of her appointment at the clinic, as I always did. I took her to the hospital and waited for her in the bustling waiting room until she had been seen for her routine check-up and was ready to leave. Usually, she emerged from the doctor's office with a big smile and chatting proudly of what the doctor told her. "I'm as fit as a fiddle for my age. The doctor said, I don't have to come back for two months." But on this occasion she waited until we were buckled into our seats and were driving out of the parking lot before she spoke.

"What did the doctor tell you this time?" I had a sinking feeling in my stomach that something was wrong but I did not want Grandmother to sense it. "The x-rays that they made on my last visit showed a huge mass in my abdomen and the doctor said that it would have to be removed surgically," she said. Staring straight ahead. I was stunned, without words for a moment. I gripped the steering wheel tightly to keep my hands from shaking. A major operation at her age! She had never been hospitalized. In fact, she seldom visited anyone in the hospital. Preferring to send one of her special handmade gifts instead. This, I thought, would be too much to have Grandmother endure.

Everyone has to go through their "Garden of Gethsemane"

"You don't have to do it if you don't want to, Grandmother." I said. "It is your decision to make not the doctor's." She turned and looked at me in surprise. "Oh I have already given my consent. I am to enter the hospital two weeks from today. Do you think I should not go through with it?" Without waiting for my answer she continued. "Like everyone else, I have to go through my 'Garden of Gethsemane.' But don't you worry, I'm not afraid." Doubt about Grandmother's decision must have been written plainly on my face as I walked her to her apartment in the senior citizen complex. Before going inside she turned to me and quoted from Psalms 31:14-15: "I trust in the Lord. My life is in His hands. Now go home and stop fretting. Where is your faith?" she scolded. The operation was an unprecedented success. Grandmother's doctors marveled at her stamina and the quick recuperative processes: and even more at her tranquility. And Grandmother, being the oldest patient in GYN at the time, was somewhat of a celebrity with other patients as well as the staff. Nurses from other wards came in to chat with her, "She is a model patient," the chief nurse commented. "Not a minute's trouble."

Within one week she was discharged from the hospital. After three weeks she was again attending Sunday morning church services. By the fourth week, Grandmother was wondering when she could resume her exercise class at the senior citizen's center.

So there was my answer shining as brightly and as clearly as the beacon of a lighthouse set high on a hill: it was Grandmother's unwavering unshakeable faith in God that made her the stalwart, strong person able to remain calm whatever the situation. She proved that. Indeed, faith can remove mountains of fear and despair that when you put your life and your affairs trustingly in God's hands you can walk through your "Garden of Gethsemane" serenely and triumphantly. I smiled as I thought "HOW SWEET IT IS!"

Grandmother Raking Leaves at 90 years of age 1990

Dayton, Ohio
April 14, 1993

Dear Grand daughter
 I dont write letters much to any one I forgot how to do so Your mother and Irene take care of Surch.. But your do so sweet I take time to Say Thank you for your Sweetness also for the cash I hope James grow his beaterful flowers

A letter from Grandmother to KV

2

Excuse this pencil and paper also poor writing I hope you keep up flower hand making I still have some of you. and my flower material

My Sister is here with f from Logan W. Va. Some one broke in on her and robed her. she is in a sad condition.

Love to James and the Children. Love from Grand mother Webster

Grandmother's Sayings and Courage

MILESTONE

Nancy Webster to turn 100 on Super Tuesday

PAGE 3

THURSDAY, MARCH 2, 2000

Dayton woman to mark 100th

Nancy Webster was born March 7, 1900

DAYTON DAILY NEWS

DAYTON — While presidential candidates and other political hopefuls are counting on Super Tuesday for a new lease on life, Nancy Webster will be counting up the years of her life.

Webster will reach centenarian status on that day. The festivities, however, begin this Saturday, when friends and family will gather to celebrate her birthday.

Nancy Webster

Webster, who was born March 7, 1900, in Boligee, Ala., was the 10th child in a family of 12. After leaving Alabama, she lived in West Virginia and Kentucky. She moved to Dayton in 1941.

From the time of her arrival here she joined the church — first, the Mount Olive Baptist Church, and later, the Corinthian Baptist Church, where she was a faithful member until illness forced her to curtail her attendance.

Webster worked many years in her church as a Sunday school teacher, and was a dedicated member of the missionary society. She is probably most remembered as the "Flower Lady," because she made corsages and arrangements for special occasions at the church.

Webster, who is a patient at Arbors of Dayton Nursing Home, will celebrate with her two daughters, Frances Moore and Irene Peavy, along with her nine grandchildren, 20 great-grandchildren and 30-plus great-great-grandchildren, and other relatives and friends from 2 to 4 p.m. Saturday at the Wesley Center.

"We thank God for this blessed privilege of having her devout and loving presence with us all of these years," Moore said.

Grandmother lived to be 101 years old

Going to the Big Rock, my memoir

Dedication

Dear Mama, Happy 90th Birthday, We are so blessed to have you in our lives. "You Light Up Our Lives" We Love You.

Kenny, Karol, Johnny, Joyce

Frances Moore's 75th Birthday Party December 1996
Joyce, Frances, Karol, Kennth, John, sitting Nancy Webster

The Big Rock

My sister, Irene, and I grew up in the hills of West Virginia where our father was a coal miner and our mother was a stay at home housewife, as was all others who lived here. After school was out for summer vacation, there was nothing for children to do as there were no parks or playgrounds or recreational centers. So we played "Soakum"(a form of baseball where a rubber ball was batted and the ball was thrown at you as you rounded the bases. If you were hit, you were out.

In addition to Soakum, we would sometimes climb the mountain for a short distance and race down, often resulting in falls that meant scuffed knees and hurt elbows. For the most part I was not involved in these pursuits as I was not considered "tomboyish" as was Irene and some of the other girls. I was more of a book worm, although there were no books available - just a *True Story* magazine that one of our aunts subscribed to. Not the most suitable reading material but I was introduced to another world - different from our situation of living without plumbing and paved roads and ice cream parlors, street cars, hotels, etc. All of which I imagined must be nice.

Our house, a three-room frame, like all the others on Walnut Hill sat facing one of the huge mountain ranges that our hollow was a part of at the very top there was a huge rock whose surface was flat and smooth like a big dinner plate or platter. I would sit on our front porch in the swing and wonder what it would be like to go to that big beautiful, smooth rock and just have a front row seat, so to speak, of the whole world. I was sure that would give me the opportunity to see how others lived away from our poor surroundings.

So one late afternoon, I decided to go to that Big Rock, as we called it. Without any planning, no lunch nor anything, I set out to climb the mountain and go see the Big Rock close up and give a big wave to all the world. But it so happened that our mother asked where I was and my sister pointed me out half-way up the hill and told her that I was going to the Big Rock. Luckily, I was not yet out of sight and happened to look back and see my mother waving frantically for me to get back down the mountain and get home. I never found out what awaited me at the top of the mountain on the big rock. But you can guess what awaited me when I came down.

A scolding that was worse than any other punishment that my mother could have given me. Believe it or not, I regret not getting to the Big Rock. Maybe that sense of adventure is the reason I chose to join a travel group that has taken me to many interesting places throughout the U. S. and also to Europe.

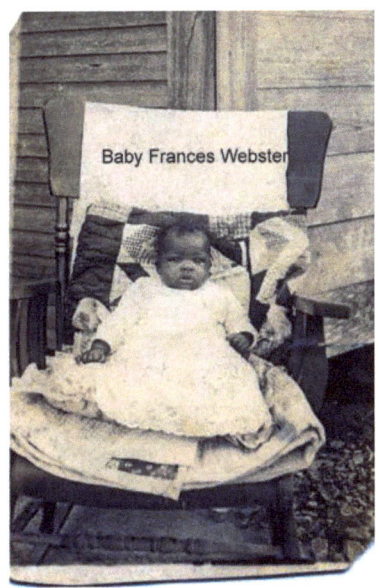

Mr. and Mrs. John W. Moss Jr.

I worked at the VA Medical Center in the Chief of Staff's office. When I retired, I started acting.

Mr. and Mrs. Jessie Moore

I later became Mrs. Jessie Moore and I a part of the Moore family

Frances Webster Moss Moore

Frances W. Moss Moore is a Contest Winner

Frances Moore one of 22 women out of thousands of applicants to win the Celebrating 60 years of Trust and Innovation Contest and was featured in a book, Celebrating 60 Years of Trust and Innovation, The science and women of PREMARIN®,(conjugated estrogens tablets, USP) 2002. Produced by Jordan Levinson. With keen interests and profound resilience, she is an inspiration at any age.

(This is her story she submitted.)

After my hysterectomy 25 years ago, my gynecologist prescribed PREMARIN®. I have been taking PREMARIN® every day for all these years, and I have never experienced any of the disturbing symptoms of menopause, like hot flashes or night sweats.

I have enjoyed excellent health and I continue to lead an active, vibrant, and invigorating life. I am always ready to face new challenges and explore new boundaries.

I have had the stamina and will to bounce back from tragedy in my life and continue to seek the good and positive things in life, while cherishing the wonderful blessings and memories of the past. In addition to my church activities, which include writing and directing various programs, I belong to a travel tour group. We toured the United States from coast to coast, as well Europe, Hawaii, and the Bahamas. Last year, a friend and I visited Paris for 7 exciting days.

I audition for TV, radio, and print media commercials (I have done 8 successfully, so far). Last year, I joined a senior acting group and performed in my first play June 2001.

I am approaching my 80th birthday with anticipation, feeling that the best is yet to be.

June 12, 2001

DAYTON DAILY NEWS 3C

THEATER REVIEW

Young at Heart Players debut

Group entertained with Coward play

By Terry Morris
Theater Critic

DAYTON — What happens to old actresses?

In the play *Waiting in the Wings*, they retire to a home for old actresses and continue to lead theatrical lives.

Others, if they're lucky, find their way into a senior citizen troupe like the Young at Heart Players, who had a successful debut last weekend at the Dayton Playhouse in the aforementioned and very suitable Noel Coward comedy.

The quality community theater production was directed by company founder Fran Pesch.

Augmented by a few younger performers, the mix of experienced and novice actors achieved a nice, comfortable blend and ensemble energy.

Sharing an ensemble experience is also one of the best things about live theater for an audience, and Coward's play provides a good opportunity.

Act 1 ends with the sweetly dangerous character Sarita Myrtle, who we've learned believes that flame is "pretty," taking a pack of matches up to her room. When the lights came up on Act 2 at Saturday night's performance, there was a shared murmur of instant recognition when the set was filled with smoke. Sarita, played by Catherine Licata, had set the place on fire, but no serious harm was done.

The cast's group spirit was especially warm during scenes that required music. Pesch's multi-talented troupe includes some players with considerable musical experience, including singer Joan Harrah, who played Bonita Belgrave, and pianist Raymonde Rougier, as Maud Melrose.

With residents like them — and others including Catherine Banks as grumpy Cora Clarke, Virginia Garcia as irascible May Davenport, Frances Moss Moore as tears-prone Estelle Craven, Dottie Wefler as fiery Deirdre O'Malley and Terry Lupp as anti-diva Lotta Bainbridge — The Wings was no mere warehouse for faded ladies of the stage with limited means.

The Young at Heart Players plan to do more productions, and take some of their shows to area festivals and community groups. For more information, call 275-1157.

➤ **Contact** Terry Morris at 225-2377, or by e-mail at terry_morris@coxohio.com

---

STILL TAKING WING.

Among the superb troupe of senior actors who performed the Noel Coward play, *Waiting in the Wings*, at the Dayton Playhouse June 8-10, was Frances Moore, who was making her theatrical debut at age 78. Mrs. Moore is no stranger to the arts. She has written plays and books and done dramatic readings and one-woman shows, but this was her first time as the member of an ensemble of actors in a formal production. The wonderful cast, most of whom were more than 70 years old, performed the play with flawless perfection — but the work turned in by Moore especially filled me with pride because, well, she's my mom.

— Khalid Moss

DDN 6-17-2001

*Mama autographed my copy of this book
Picture from the Celebrating 60 years of Trust and Innovation*

OH YES YOU ARE A ROLE MODEL FOR ALL OF US!!

90th Birthday Party

And now we are celebrating your 90th Birthday, December 16, 2011. The Mosses, Peavys, Moores, other family members and friends gather together to celebrate your life beyond midlife.

Please join us to celebrate our mother,
Frances Moss Moore,
on her 90th Birthday!

Where: The Dayton Grand Hotel
11 S. Ludlow Street, Dayton, Ohio
Date: Saturday, December 17, 2011
Time: 1:00 to 4:00 PM

After the party, visit

BROWN TONES PUBLISHING

www.harriettubmanbooks.com

To see pictures and to share your memories

www.ingramcontent.com/pod-product-compliance
Lightning Source LLC
Chambersburg PA
CBHW041641090426
42736CB00034BA/1